A World of Difference

Dianne Young

Whitecap Books

Vancouver/Toronto

To Kendra

Edited by Elaine Jones
Proofread by Elizabeth McLean
Cover and interior design by Warren Clark
Photo credits: Thomas Kitchin/First Light p. 4, 12, 15, 16, 23, 27; Darwin Wiggett/First Light p. 7; K. Aitken/First Light p. 8, 20; Florian Graner/Innerspace Visions p. 11; D & J Heaton/First Light p. 19; Jean B. Heguy/First Light p. 24; Erwin & Peggy Bauer/First Light p. 28; Bill Dow/First Light p. 31.

Printed and bound in Canada

Canadian Cataloguing in Publication Data

Young, Dianne, 1959-
     A world of difference
     (A which is which book)

     ISBN 1-55110-955-7

     1. Animals—Identification—Juvenile literature. I. Title. II. Series.
QL49.Y68 1999   j591   C99-910848-9

The publisher acknowledges the support of the Canada Council for the Arts and the Cultural Services Branch of the Government of British Columbia for our publishing program. We acknowledge the financial support of the Government of Canada through the Book Industry Development Program for our publishing activities.

It's easy to tell the difference between a rabbit and a dolphin. They don't look much alike at all! But can you tell the difference between a rabbit and a hare? Or a dolphin and a porpoise?

Look at the pictures in this book, and see if you can guess "which is which." Is that an elk or a caribou? A bobcat or a Canada lynx? Read on to see if you were right, and check out the other fun facts. Just how big is a baby elephant when it's born?

Have fun!

WHICH IS WHICH ?

Is this a rabbit or a hare?

If you could have seen this animal when it was born, it would have been easy to tell which it was. Rabbits are born helpless, with no hair and with their eyes closed. Hares can hop around on their own soon after birth. They do have hair and their eyes are open.

But this animal wasn't just born. Is there any other way to tell which it is?

As winter approaches and the days become shorter, most types of hares that live in snowy climates change from brown to white. Rabbits never change color. They remain brown or gray, even in winter.

So if you guessed that it was a hare, you were right!

"As mad as a March hare" is how people might describe someone who is acting silly or goofy. Why? March is the breeding season for many rabbits and hares, and they do behave oddly then. They often leap up in the air, and even stand on their hind legs and box!

Rabbit

Jackrabbits aren't rabbits—they're hares! They were originally called jackass rabbits, because their huge ears look like the ears on a jackass, which is a male donkey.

WHICH IS WHICH ?

Is this a dolphin or a porpoise?

The best way to tell the difference between a dolphin and a porpoise is by their teeth. Dolphins have cone-shaped teeth, while porpoises have teeth with flat tops.

But what if you don't get to play dentist with a dolphin or porpoise? Is there another way to tell these two apart?

An easier, but not foolproof, way is to see whether or not it has a beak—a long, slightly pointed part at the front of its head. *Most* dolphins have beaks but *no* porpoises have beaks. Since this creature *does* have a beak, it *can't* be a porpoise.

So if you guessed that it was a dolphin, you were right!

Dolphins and porpoises are mammals, not fish!
- They give birth to their babies. (Fish lay eggs.)
- They are warm-blooded. Their body temperature stays about the same no matter how warm or cold the water is. (Fish are cold-blooded. Their body temperature changes with the water temperature.)
- They get oxygen by breathing air into their lungs. (Fish get oxygen by passing water through their gills.)

A group of dolphins or porpoises is called a gam, or a pod.

WHICH IS WHICH?

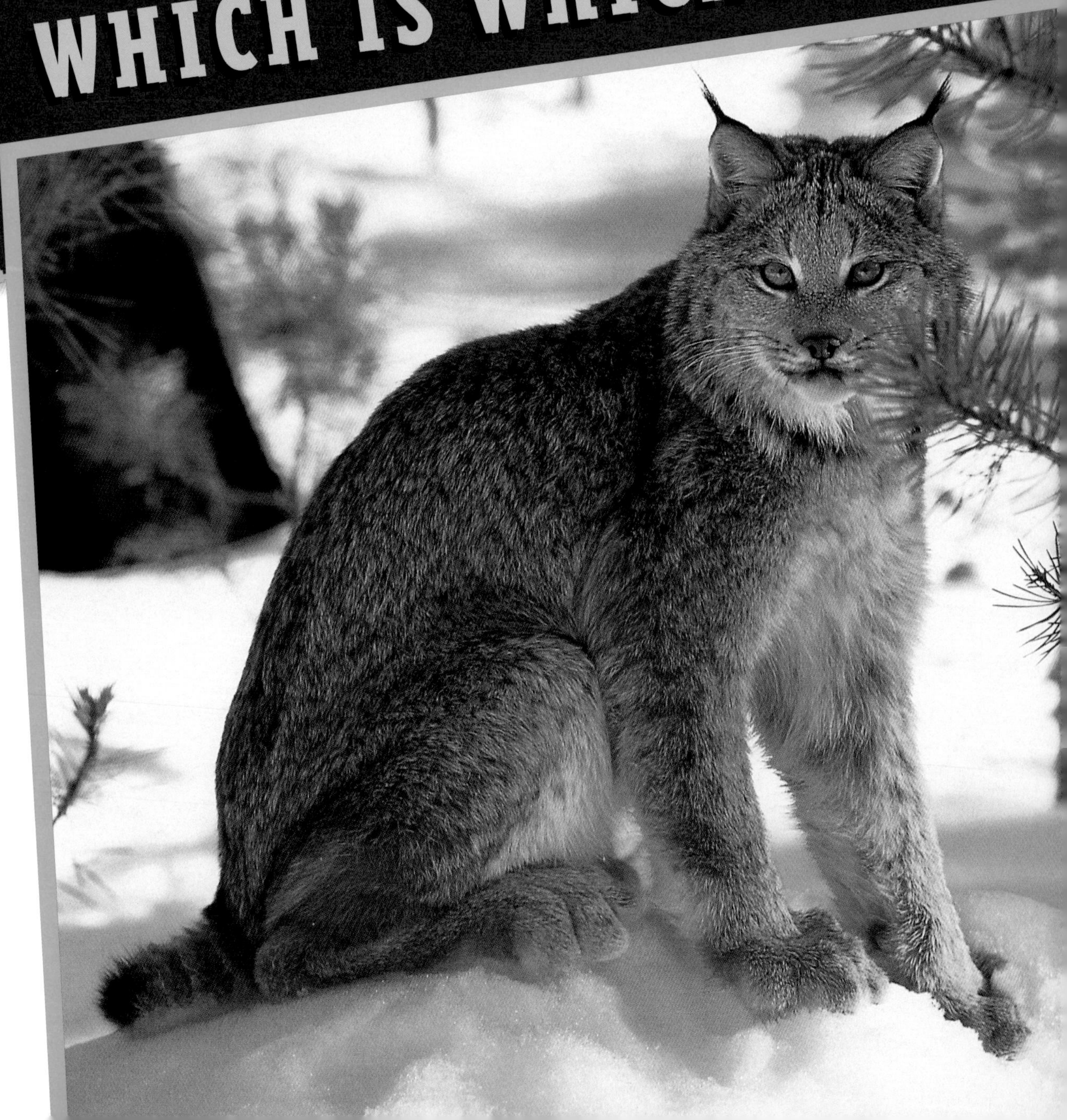

Is this a bobcat or a Canada lynx?

Both animals look like very big house cats. They have tufts of black hair on the tips of their ears and ruffs of hair on the sides of their faces. They both have short tails. So what's the difference between them?

A bobcat has paws that look the right size for its body. A Canada lynx has huge paws that look far too big for it. They act as built-in snowshoes in winter.

But its feet may be hidden in snow or grasses. Don't worry. There is another way to tell these two apart.

Both the bobcat and the Canada lynx have short tails, but the ends of their tails look different. The tip of a bobcat's tail is black on top and white on the bottom. The tip of a Canada lynx's tail is black all the way around.

So if you guessed that it was a Canada lynx, you were right!

Bobcats eat many different small animals, but Canada lynxes prefer one particular animal— the snowshoe hare.

Bobcats and Canada lynxes have excellent night vision. We need six times more light to see than they do!

Bobcat

Is this an Asian or an African elephant?

This is definitely an elephant, but what kind of elephant is it? An Asian elephant has one triangle-shaped "finger" on the end of its trunk, on the top. An African elephant has two "fingers" on the end of its trunk, one on the top, and the other on the bottom.

But its trunk may be in the water—or in its mouth. Is there any other way to tell them apart?

L ook at the size of their ears. An Asian elephant's ears are shorter from top to bottom than its head is. An African elephant's ears are longer than its head.

So if you guessed that it was an African elephant, you were right!

A newborn baby elephant is a little taller than your kitchen counter and weighs as much as your refrigerator!

One of an elephant's tusks is usually worn down more than the other. Elephants are "right-tusked" or "left-tusked," just like people are right-handed or left-handed!

Asian elephant

Is this a fur seal or a sea lion?

If you could feel this animal's coat, it would be easy to tell which it was. Fur seals have a thick soft coat of fur, while sea lions have only a thin coat of hair.

But it's pretty hard to tell from the picture what kind of coat this animal has, isn't it? Don't worry. There is still another way to tell fur seals and sea lions apart.

Fur seals have a pointed snout, and sea lions have a blunt snout. Look back and you'll see that the other animal's snout is definitely pointed.

So if you guessed that it was a fur seal, you were right!

Fur seals and sea lions belong to a group of animals called "pinnipeds" because they have flippers rather than arms or legs. Pinniped means fin-footed.

Sea lions

Adult male seals and sea lions are called bulls, and adult females are called cows, but their babies are *not* called calves—they are called pups!

24

Is this an elk or a caribou?

An elk has antlers that look a little like branches on a tree. Each branch, called a "tine," comes to a point. The branches of a caribou's antlers get wider at the end and have many smaller rounded points on them. They look something like hands, with wide palms and very short fingers. In fact, this kind of antler is called "palmate."

But elk and caribou both shed their antlers every year. Is there a way to tell them apart when they don't have antlers?

The easiest way to tell an elk and a caribou apart is by their color. An elk is brown with a darker neck and legs. A caribou is lighter colored even on its neck and legs. They also look different from the rear. An elk has a large tan or white patch on its rump. The caribou has only a small white patch under its tail.

So if you guessed that it was an elk, you were right!

Another name for elk is *wapiti*, a Native American word meaning "white rump."

Caribou

You can hear a clicking sound when a caribou walks because of the way tendons (cords of tissue that connect muscles to bones) snap across bones in the lower part of its legs.

Is this a jaguar, a leopard or a cheetah?

You're admiring this big spotted cat at the zoo, but so are a lot of other people and they're standing in front of the sign! Is this a leopard or a jaguar or a cheetah?

Suddenly, the cat lets out a roar! That narrows your choices down, because leopards and jaguars can roar, but cheetahs can't. So this has to be either a leopard or a jaguar. But how can you tell which it is?

29

You can tell by its spots. The spots on both leopards and jaguars form broken circles called rosettes, but jaguars also have a spot or two in the center of each rosette. A cheetah's spots, by the way, are solid dark circles.

So if you guessed that it was a jaguar, you were right!

Cheetahs are the fastest land animals— they can run faster than a car travels on the highway! But unlike cars, cheetahs can only go this fast for a very short time.

Leopard

Cheetahs may not be able to roar, but they can do something that leopards and jaguars can't—they can purr!

Index